SHARING
YOUR
STORY

Marketing Your Book
Without the
~~Hard Sell~~

MICHELLE WORTHINGTON

Published by Share Your Story Australia 2018

Copyright © 2018 Michelle Worthington

sharingyourstory.com.au

A catalogue record for this book is available from the National Library of Australia.

Book cover design and formatting services by BookCoverCafe.com

ISBN:
978-0-6482270-0-7 (pbk)
978-0-6482270-1-4 (e-bk)

Contents

Introduction: Share Your Story v

SECTION 1 Follow the Yellow Brick Road: 1
Start the Process
1 Develop Your Story 3
2 Develop Your Business Plan 7
3 Develop Your Marketing Plan 10
4 Develop Your Brand 13
5 Develop Your Mindset 16

SECTION 2 Purpose Is Everything: Story 19
6 Give Yourself a Mission and a Purpose 21
7 Make Your Plan Relevant and Specific 25
8 Be More Attractive 28

SECTION 3 Authors as Entrepreneurs: Business Plan 31
9 Be Your Business 33
10 Set Your Goalposts 38
11 Have Team Spirit 40
12 Know the Playground, the Players and the Game 42

13 Talk the Talk; Walk the Walk   46
14 Celebrate the Little Wins   51

SECTION 4 The Power of the Backstory: 53
Marketing Plan
15 Putting the Social into Social Media   55
16 Post with Purpose   59
17 Like. Comment. Share.   63
18 Don't Believe the Hype   67

SECTION 5 Bringing it Together: Brand   73
19 Who Exactly Are You?   75
20 Why Do I Need to Do This?   79
21 When Should I Start?   86
22 Where Can I Promote Myself?   89

SECTION 6 You Had the Power All Along,   93
My Dear: Mindset
23 Be Relentlessly Resilient   95
24 Sharing Is Caring   100
25 Build It and They Will Come   103
26 Learn from the Best   106
27 The Right Book, the Right Time, the Right Person   110

About the Author   115

Introduction: Share Your Story

B orn and bred in Brisbane, I showed real promise as an author as a child. I told myself stories and loved getting lost in books. My best friends from childhood were characters from the stories I read. Winner of the 1988 Little Swaggie Award and other Australian poetry competitions, I had poems published in numerous Australian and international anthologies.

From a very early age, I had a love of words and rhyme, and have always excelled at English and creative writing, graduating with a Bachelor of Arts from the University of Queensland in 1996. All I ever really wanted to do was write, but life got in the way. I thought I had loads of time. I was wrong.

A grain of experience is worth a ton of theory. When I was growing up, I wanted to be an English teacher, helping others fall in love with words like

I had. After being mercilessly bullied at school for being pint-sized and smart, you would hardly think that coming back to school to work for the rest of my life would be a goal. In fact, after the bullying continued in high school, teaching did become the furthest thing from my mind and I gave up on my dream.

I learnt to hide how smart I was so I didn't get beaten up on the way home, or lose my friends, who thought I was showing off. I just couldn't figure out the purpose of being smart if it didn't help me or anyone else.

I went to university and double majored in coffee shop, then life got in the way and still I never followed my passion for teaching. In a way, that was a blessing. I learnt far more from the school of hard knocks about what it means to be a teacher and coach than I would have doing formal study.

At the core of it all, I wanted to help people. I love seeing people's dreams come true. I love seeing people discover that they are so much more than what they thought they could or would be.

I'm passionate about sharing my love of words with the next generation of readers and storytellers. I love talking about engaging special-needs kids through sensory storytelling; writing and publishing picture books in which all children can see their reflections; and encouraging new voices in children's writing.

My vision for the world is that all children have access to books that mirror their own lives, which introduce them to the endless possibilities that are theirs for the taking.

When my first son was born, it reignited my passion to get a book published. I started sending unedited copies of poems to publishers, without any research or any idea about what it meant to be published. I made unsolicited submissions, like the majority of aspiring authors. It took me ten years to get my first book published. I don't want other people to make the same mistakes I did. I want to help them publish their books in an easier and better way.

When I discovered the business side of publishing, marketing and promotion weren't my strong points. I had no idea where to start, but I didn't think I could sell my books the same way a bank sells its services, or party plans sell makeup. I was sure it involved a much more refined process, being that writing was such an illustrious career.

I had so much to give. I wanted to help aspiring authors not make the same mistakes I had. Although I didn't have the opportunity to speak at writers' festivals or workshops, I knew I had something to say. I had information that could help the people in those audiences.

I decided to start my own business, called Share Your Story, with the aim of helping as many authors as possible get their books published. I wanted to help authors learn about the publishing industry as a business by connecting them with professionals, within the publishing industry and elsewhere, that could help them on their journey to becoming successful writers, whatever that looked like for them.

People buy books from those they know, or those they would like to know. When the story behind the story is shared, an audience is created that is invested in the success of the writer. That's why I called my business *Share Your Story*.

The business has given me the platform I need to help other authors realise their dreams of seeing their stories in print. It is based on the principles of honesty, resilience, persistence, the sharing of knowledge, and passion. I believe everyone should have the opportunity to share their story, which should be judged on its own merit and published for the good it can do the world rather than how much money it makes.

I am an advocate for diversity in children's writing and publishing, and an ambassador for promoting new voices in the arts. But I soon discovered that I was only giving writers half of the skills they needed. I wanted to further limit the amount of effort they expended to achieve success.

Authors in the community that I had helped get traditional publishing contracts, or start their own publishing companies, were still frustrated. It wasn't as easy to sell their books as they had been led to believe. They were being told how to get published, but not about what came afterwards.

I'm always open and honest about how hard I've worked to get where I am and in everything I do, and I wanted my clients to benefit from my experience.

I get frustrated when my message doesn't seem to be reaching enough people, or, if it does, they don't understand the importance of hard work and planning to get the results they want.

I get frustrated when I can't grow my business as fast as I would like.

I get frustrated when publishing companies make decisions on manuscripts based on what sells, not on what stories need to be told to represent all the diverse aspects of the world.

I get frustrated when a badly written book gets an award for being a bestseller, yet there are not enough grants, writing competitions or funds to develop emerging talent in the arts.

I started my own business because I wanted aspiring authors to get the real story behind being published. It became very clear to me that I needed to improve the way I was marketing my books, and myself as an author. It's very hard to get invited to speak at writing festivals and workshops unless you're well known and widely published. I wasn't being offered the speaking opportunities I needed to grow my platform, so I decided to start my own.

Most guest speakers I had listened to spoke from the *end* of the process, not the beginning, and I knew that's what authors needed to know. There were no workshops that covered the challenges authors face when they're just starting their publishing journey; the difference between traditional marketing and online marketing; and the countless changes occurring within the industry.

It was hard work learning event planning and marketing. I wanted to get my message across, in an interactive setting, to the people I thought needed it the most, and the concept was exactly what people were looking for. In the twelve months since I started, my business has grown to where I have tribe members from all over Australia and throughout the world.

It's just me. I am a small-business owner. Within three months of changing my mindset, when I started to think of myself as a small-business owner and consultant to aspiring authors rather than 'just a picture-book author', I quit my day job to focus on promotion and marketing full time.

I started to attend networking and business events, where at first I felt totally out of my league. My small, home-based business was still in start-up stage, and when I told people what I did for a living their eyes glazed over. I could see them looking around for a *real* businessperson to talk to. I wasn't even on their radar as someone worthy of being a business contact, let alone someone who could possibly help them in business. It was embarrassing, heartbreaking—and exactly what I needed. It gave me the strength to move my business to the next level.

SECTION 1

Follow the Yellow Brick Road:

Start the Process

1. Develop your story
2. Develop your business plan
3. Develop your marketing plan
4. Develop your brand
5. Develop your mindset

Chapter 1

Develop Your Story

My first business, Michelle Worthington – Author, was created when I made a conscious effort to get my manuscript published. It was ten years before I saw my story in print. At first I thought it was because it simply wasn't good enough. Then a publishing company offered me a contract, but that fell through due to cutbacks during the global financial crisis. The main reason it took me so long was that I had no idea what I was doing, where I should start, or who I could ask for help.

My journey to publication has been an educational, empowering, enriching experience, but at first I didn't have the business skills required to start making money from it. There was so much more to writing books than I could ever have imagined. I had to become a small-business owner to promote and market my books if I wanted to be successful. I then made it my business to help other authors by connecting them with industry professionals, which enabled them to have a more positive experience on their own paths to becoming authors. This led to my creating my second business, Share Your Story.

It was through this experience that I learnt the difference between achieving financial security and getting rich quick. Achieving financial security involves commitment, responsibility and respect for money. Getting rich quick often involves a high level of risk for an often-temporary gain. Choosing which of these principals to apply when starting your business is up to you, but you will come to know, as I have, that making money from the sales of your book, whether you publish traditionally or independently, is a tremendously hard enterprise. Unless you appreciate the journey towards success, you will not appreciate what you have when you get there, and the money you do make from your sales will never feel like enough.

When your natural need for following your passion is realised, making money will become less of an issue and you can focus your attention on other areas of your business. Wealth is not required to do great things for others. It is the doing, not the having, that makes a person rich.

It became clear to me very quickly that book publishing is, first and foremost, a business. It exists to make money. No large or small business is immune from the influence of politics, and the rising costs of housing, healthcare, childcare and education, as well as changes in the economy. This has left many hardworking authors struggling to make a profit.

Using the information and processes that I learnt through trial and error, I came to the conclusion that it's possible to craft a successful career from *any* small business. Why should being an author be any different? Like me, you may pass through different phases on your journey to success, finding new ways to market your book without the hard sell.

Share Your Story was founded to educate authors on getting published, but it grew to include authors in small business that needed to be informed and educated in order to set realistic goals, and create long-term business plans.

I know it feels like no one notices you, the quiet person in the corner who looks a little tired. No one sees how hard you try and how much effort you put into your work. Sometimes they only seem to notice when you make a mistake or can't keep up anymore. I see you, and I know what you're going through. Every day you get up and do what you can do, and that's enough.

Remember, it's hard to put a value on your story when you're constantly measuring yourself against someone else's success. When you feel discouraged, you need to celebrate the smallest milestones, even if they go unrecognised by others. Remember also that it's the little things that are the most important and worth paying attention to.

Chapter 2

Develop Your Business Plan

Even though I had worked in the banking industry for over twenty years, it still took me some time to get my business plan in order. Your business plan will depend on your motivation. Are you writing a book to realise your goal of being a full-time author, like me? Or do you want to gain credibility as a published author on a topic of influence and write a book to provide an alternate source of income, like this one?

My author-business model has three main elements:

1. Books
2. Business
3. Branding

If you're writing a book to establish your writing journey, be aware that the business model you create should allow you time to both produce and promote, otherwise it will affect the momentum of your career instead of advancing it.

If you're writing a book to promote your business, factor it into your business model, including the time it will take to produce and promote, otherwise it will affect the momentum of your business instead of advancing it.

If you unhook the pendulum of a clock, the inner workings will keep going for a while, but they will soon run down. Draw on the power of your already solid business plan, or create a new pendulum that makes time for your writing.

There is a world of art, poetry, science, religion and philosophy to inspire you, but there is also a place for being business minded. If you have trouble putting into words what you would like to create, consider your mind as a picture gallery where you keep images of what you want your book to look like. If you're creating what you want deliberately, you will be expressing the real truth about you and your purpose, and it will come naturally to you. This will be much more genuine than writing for the ever-changing circumstances of trends in business, and the publishing industry.

Chapter 3

Develop Your Marketing Plan

Your book-marketing plan should focus more on discoverability than selling. Your work is important, so instead of selling your book in the general marketplace it's better to make it more accessible to those who can benefit from it.

Marketing is the answer to every financial problem. Sustainability in business, or as a full-time author, can only be achieved with a comprehensive and effective marketing campaign. High-quality work will only take you so far if your target market doesn't know about it.

Community development, alternate income streams, and more clients in more places, more often and more efficiently can only be achieved through marketing. Functional activities around day-to-day running of the business and organic promotion need to become second nature so they are no longer the blockers that are stopping you from growing your business and brand. Instead, they should form a foundation you can build on.

Writing a well-crafted, engaging and appealing book is the first and main focus of any successful book-marketing plan. A well-written book, no matter how compelling, will still struggle to sell if the target audience doesn't know your book exists.

Researching and reaching a specific target audience is the first step in promoting your book without the hard sell. If your book is so in tune with the needs and wants of the audience you have written it for, it will hardly be a struggle at all for them to see the benefit in having it on their bookshelves.

This is much harder to achieve than it sounds, however. Most small businesses struggle to find the funds to spend on marketing and promotion, much less the time to find beta readers for potential manuscripts, or assets to research a niche segment.

For a book to be successful, this is the area of a business-and-marketing plan that requires the most creative thinking and ingenuity. Whether you are traditionally or independently published, ensuring that your book is professionally edited, formatted and designed is crucial to creating a product that will give you credibility. Having your book professionally edited, proofread and designed is crucial to creating a product that will give you credibility. In effect, it will become your business card in many networking situations.

Chapter 4

Develop Your Brand

Bringing your business and marketing plans together, and incorporating both into your author brand, will help explain what you are working on, not only to your target market, but also to yourself. Your business and marketing strategies show how you plan to do the work; your author brand explains why what you do matters.

You're going to have challenges along the way, so it's important to remind yourself every day of what your stories mean to you, and what they can help you achieve.

Developing a brand will help you capture the attention of your target market and, as a side effect, sell more books.

Knowing your audience before you engage with them is key to ensuring that you're adding value to their lives with your book. You have the luxury of choosing who you want to work with, and where and when you want work, because your *why* gives you the credentials to do so. The only way to truly know your audience is to put yourself out there and meet them.

It's worth taking the time to get to know the people that you hope will become your most enthusiastic fans. You know you have a great business, deep expertise, and that you can make a difference, but you will be frustrated if you can't find your readers. In most cases, you know how much better their lives could be because you have had the same experiences. You simply want to share what you leaned.

Remember, as an author you are your *brand*, not your books. Not everyone is part of your target market, and generic, all-purpose promotion will be a waste of your precious time. Find the people who will benefit the most from knowing you and reading your book, and then build your brand based on who and what you want to be known for.

Get to know your readers and let them get to know you. Start with common ground before you add twists and turns that take them into unknown territory. This advice holds for every genre in publishing, and not just nonfiction. In order to tell a story, the first rule is to start at the beginning.

Grow your author brand from a place of gratitude. As an author and the owner of your own small business, you have the luxury of interacting with the people you want to work with. And although your target market is always your main concern, you should also consider the communities that will benefit from your time and support. Do what you can do with diligence, learn to say no when there's something you can't do, and remember to take the time to breathe.

You could also consider what would make a difference to the lives of those around you. Sales are also often a side effect of gratitude so don't be afraid to attract a following by offering service and help to your peers.

Chapter 5

Develop Your Mindset

A peculiarity of the human mind is its desire to see things clearly in the most clean-cut outlines, so that there is no mistaking what they are. As a businessperson, you are able to assign things in proper proportion. As an author, you can see things as they really are rather than distorted by your pain and survival instincts. You can learn to appreciate the blessings you never knew you had, and to see the problems of the life you had been leading.

Once you have a clear direction, part of that clarity comes with a responsibility to help others achieve the same. If you don't practise a positive mindset on a regular basis, you can lose sight of the bigger picture.

If you focus only on your own success, you may give up before you get to that sweet spot where all the past trials and tribulations have finally begun to make sense. Then you can journey down the right path towards your dreams, confident in the knowledge that you now have all the experience you need to be a game changer in your industry. Change the game for the better.

I light up when I am part of a learning experience, whether I am part of a workshop or with my mentor clients, when the right information is given to the right person at the right time—when they are open and ready to receive it. I am always so proud when I see writers who are brave enough to share their stories with strangers for the first time. It is as though they have been released from their own limitations, and they come alive with the knowledge that they can be just as glorious as they knew they could be.

I light up when I have the ways and means to help others, either by spending time with them, or by sharing my story and giving them what is mine to give for the sole purpose of changing their lives for the better.

By giving of myself, I am infinitely more fulfilled, more energised and more empowered than I ever would be if I focused on sales alone. By sharing my story, I have the opportunity to shine my light out into the world, like a lighthouse that will attract those who need my guidance the most.

If you want to be genuinely successful, becoming a published author isn't simply about selling a book as a means of generating an alternate passive income stream. Success is only one link to the world around you. Adopting an organic marketing plan and a giveback mindset will lead to permanent and progressive change in your business. By sharing your story without the hard sell, you will foster long-term relationships with your community, and forge mutually beneficial professional connections that will give back to you in expediential quantities.

Sharing your story in your own words, in your own way, from a place of purpose is worth more than you can imagine.

SECTION 2

Purpose Is Everything:

Story

Chapter 6

Give Yourself a Mission and a Purpose

If you have just started in the publishing industry and want to make a career as a full-time author, your only credibility comes from your capability. Publishing companies and other authors need to see you as an equal. They need to understand what you do, and your current level of authority, as well as your future capabilities.

This won't happen overnight. To increase your credibility, you need to make the commitment to stay the distance in the publishing industry, even when things get tough. The more credibility you have, the easier it will be to market your brand and promote your books. Unless you are resilient and solid in your business purpose and plan, you will give up before you reach the time in your writing career when things get easier.

1. Write a mission statement. Here is mine for Share Your Story: *By focusing on my strengths, my customers, and my underlying values, my business profit will double every year, while adding value to my life. My business has a step-by-step plan for increasing income and improving profitability. The amount of money that flows from my business is in harmony with its balance-sheet capabilities. My business pays the bills on time, providing creditors with the loyalty and sound economics of an astute business partner. My business plan gives my clients the assurance that I will always be there when they need me. This is my career.*

2. Do a mind map of how your business will be structured. Demonstrate the cash flow, but also include what you yourself will do and what you will delegate. What do you want to achieve? You've spent all your time getting your head around the concept of becoming an author, but now you also have to starting thinking like a businessperson; you must become a marketing specialist as well as a creative genius.

Getting noticed is the end goal, but what do you want to be known for? And how will you achieve that?

3. Do an analysis of why any previous business or publications failed to succeed, and establish clear rules on what you will do differently this time.

4. Dedicate your author business to delivering quality products, and never lose sight of the importance of good service. Your experience will suffer if the assistance you give others, and yourself, is not of the highest standard. This may mean investing time and money in yourself to ensure you become the best brand ambassador possible.

5. Market yourself as well as your books. Be open to new and exciting ways to increase the flow of money into your life

6. Follow good management practices. Accurate inventory, sound accounting practices, and quality control are all necessary to maintain a positive cash flow.

When you take good care of your business, your business will take good care of you. When you know exactly where you stand financially, you will create solid foundations for all other aspects of your life. Learn how to be confident and practical in making financial decisions. Use knowledge to combat confusion, and it will follow that managing your money becomes more bearable, interesting and reassuring.

As a business owner, you are the CEO of a family-owned and family-run business, no matter what size it is. Money will flow in and out. Money will flow to you in gratitude for your hard work. Money will flow out to support your quality of life. Accept that you are now a small-business owner and your book alone may not be good enough to sell itself. Marketing without the hard sell is about asking and answering the questions that no one else is addressing, asking for feedback from your target market to confirm you are on the right track, and investing your time in what takes your author business forward. Look at what makes the people you admire in other industries successful, and adapt what works into your own author-business plan.

Chapter 7

Make Your Plan Relevant and Specific

Develop a plan that is perfectly suited to your needs and wants. Give your goals real meaning. Use your inner talents, passions and goals to determine how you will delegate your time and assets. Ask yourself:

- What is important?
- What makes my life better?
- What am I good at?
- How am I different?
- What do I get excited about?
- What do I need to do?
- What is my true worth?

Make it specific:

- Take control of your time by using a diary effectively; make the best use of your time by doing things that work.
- Create a daily to-do list. Take a few minutes at the end of each day to write down what you plan to do the following day. This will help you evaluate how much of your day is available for business use, and how much time to set aside for non-negotiable family time. This is not a time to complain about not having enough hours in the day; use your time more effectively by making the task of setting priorities and planning with purpose a daily habit.
- Use a weekly timetable to provide a detailed account of your activities; use it to map all regular activities, including family, work and leisure.
- Use a yearly planner for important dates and deadlines, such as submission dates, editor deadlines, and launches. Make sure you schedule extracurricular activities such as appointments or family commitments on the same calendar to show how your business fits within the family framework.
- Schedule time for the family; this is non-negotiable.

Authors and business owners make a grave mistake if they don't use commonsense when formulating their author-business plan. Know your limitations, which are often other people's priorities and demands on your time, and factor them into what you can achieve right now. Also, consider how that can change to make more time for writing and marketing in the future.

We can view most things in one of two ways: from either an emotional or sentimental point of view, or a hard, commonsense business way. When it comes to a holistic business plan, it's more practical and sensible to look at things in both ways, allowing commonsense to decide whether decisions are made with the head or the heart.

Whether your business plan is in your head or your bottom drawer, or on your computer, it is very unlikely that a backer will give you a call out of the blue to ask if you have products or books they could help you promote. Make your plan visible. Share it on social media. Ensure that your business plan is inclusive, transparent, adaptable, and wired towards achieving the goals you have set for you and your family.

Chapter 8

Be More Attractive

Your life ought to be most beautiful and attractive thing in the world to you. If it is, it will attract like-minded people. If you want to win some, you must be winsome. You not only have knowledge, you have experience. Every truth spoken, and every message given to the world, is borne of your own reality. Become the kind of person that people are attracted to for your inner light and uniqueness.

What are you doing to attract or repel the people around you? People want to work with me because I'm honest and open about my journey. They are looking for something more because they feel unfulfilled. They know there must be more to life, and they may want to leave a legacy. Proud of their families, they want to be good role models. I have the same goals.

They worry about money and having enough time to do everything they want to do. They worry about the future, and that life won't live up to their expectations. It annoys them that they have to make a living doing something they don't love. It keeps them up at night when they stress about how they are going to make money by following their dreams, and how other people will react and judge them. That has been my life over the past twenty years.

They are happy when they're being creative. They are sad when they're feeling unheard and passed over. They want to be validated as real business owners. A job that pays the bills is a means to an end, and they know that's not the reason they were put on Earth. They are not fulfilling their destiny.

What attracts these people to me is that I have walked in their shoes. In fact, I'm walking the same road right now, but I'm just a little way ahead. Social media allows me to show potential readers and tribe members where I am in my journey, and offers them the opportunity not only to share it with me but also to learn from it.

SECTION 3

Authors as Entrepreneurs:

Business Plan

Chapter 9

Be Your Business

This book is designed to assist authors through a 5-step framework that will develop a business mindset in order to get the most leverage from their marketing plan. I developed the framework after working with individuals and groups to streamline the process for promoting a book without taking creative introverts too far out of their comfort zone.

The first part of the process is to develop an author-business plan. The moment an author signs a book contract to independently publish their book, they are a small-business owner. This can often be the biggest hurdle to success for writers, and can keep them from turning their passion into a profession.

Be relevant and specific about whom you are and what you want to achieve. You don't need to start your own company by helping others, but you do need to think about your own products—that is, your books—as being produced and promoted as part of your business. Having a big-picture mindset will move your writing career further than simply reacting to the ups and downs of the industry.

Example: Executive summary

Group workshops are designed in partnership with book professionals and incorporate success stories to best suit writers who are new to the world of publishing as well as making them cutting edge, dynamic and inclusive in a fast-changing industry.

Mentor programs will be tailored to the specific need of the participant.

Manuscript editing and assessment will be conducted by industry professionals, and will give an insight into which pathway to publication would be most suited to each particular manuscript.

The corporate market for events that empower authors is strong, even though most authors do not want to spend large amounts of money on personal and writing development. They recognise that investing in training from published authors of influence, and access to shared resources, is always a good investment.

Share Your Story intends to honour the promise of community engagement by allocating a portion of each income stream to international literacy programs and international book-giving programs, as well as providing face-to-face support and fundraising for local charities.

Additionally, Share Your Story aims to empower students so they can engage with their peers as future workshop presenters, editors or mentors when they have achieved their own level of success.

Share Your Story's projected growth rate will be over one hundred percent by the end of year three, and will have profits as a function of sales of over eleven percent by year three. By the beginning of year two, Share Your Story will have three employees.

Mission

The mission of the Share Your Story is to provide authors with the highest level of self-empowerment through education, and help them achieve their goal of publication. We exist to attract and promote authors. Our services will exceed the expectations of our authors. We have a mission to work towards the United Nationals Global Goals for Sustainable Development by supporting disadvantaged people, both locally and internationally.

Objectives

Share Your Story's objectives for the first three years of operation:

1. Create a service-based company whose #1 goal for authors is to get their work published.
2. Utilise our services so we can donate to charitable companies.
3. Increase our number of published authors by twenty percent per year through superior educational programs.
4. Publish nonfiction books as an alternative income stream, and a way of raising founder profile.
5. Develop a sustainable, profitable small business.

Michelle Worthington is an award-winning, internationally published author, and the creator and director of Share Your Story. Share Your Story is a resource for authors specialising in education, personal empowerment and community engagement. Share Your Story will offer three types of educational services: group workshops, mentor programs, and manuscript editing and assessment. The educational services will be either author-development training or author-skills training.

Chapter 10

Set Your Goalposts

You will need to create a definition of yourself as your own company. Authors very rarely make a living from royalties alone. By expanding how you think of yourself, your talents and your skill set, you will be diversifying the income streams that will help you grow your author business. Write down what you do now and what you aspire to do.

Company ownership

Michelle Worthington will trade under the registered business name of Share Your Story. The business has an ABN.

Start-up summary

Share Your Story start-up costs will include all the necessary equipment needed to set up a home office, and fees for business registration, accounting, online advertising, and website-development.

The home office equipment will include a laptop computer, which will be installed with Microsoft Office and anti-virus software. The accounting fees will pay for a professional accountant. The business registration fees will be used for the trading name. The online advertising costs will be based on the need to communicate services to perspective customers, and will be predominately Facebook ads promoting the events. The web creation fees at start-up will be for the creation of the website www.sharingyourstory.com.au.

Example: Company summary

Michelle Worthington, author, will produce quality books of all genres for a contemporary market. As the director of Share Your Story, she will offer consultancy services to authors who want to publish their books. Share Your Story will specialise in training workshops, mentor programs, and manuscript assessment. Share Your Story is a home-based business located in Brisbane. Share Your Story will begin making a profit after month thirteen, and will grow steadily each consecutive month thereafter.

Chapter 11

Have Team Spirit

What other skills do you have other than writing great books? Is there a way you can promote yourself to the industry as someone who can and will share their knowledge with the next generation of authors? As authors, by sharing our stories we not only entertain; we also empower and inspire.

Example: Services

Group workshops will be used for two different reasons. They will either be educational workshops run by published authors, or training-skills workshops run by industry professionals.

Mentor programs will provide personalised education programs based on the specific needs of each client. While Share Your Story's core competencies are not in teaching authors how to write, the business will align itself with well-respected writers' groups and make authors aware of their services. By using strategic partnerships, Share Your Story will maintain a narrow focus while still offering participants the information they need.

Manuscript editing and assessment, conducted by experienced editors with industry experience, are online services where manuscripts are uploaded via the business website. These services will be open to international authors. They will make our local services visible, as well as provide validation and feedback to authors all over the world. We will also provide information and advice for a possible pathway to publication.

Michelle Worthington will offer educational and consultancy services to authors through Share Your Story, and will concentrate on three types of programs: group workshops, mentor programs, and manuscript editing and assessment.

Chapter 12

Know the Playground, the Players and the Game

If you want to win at any game, you need to know the rules. The publishing industry is continually evolving, and the framework within which authors work can change based on countless economic and technological shifts and bends to meet the industry's immediate needs. By knowing how the industry has been operating in the past, being aware of industry trends, understanding who are the major players, knowing who your team mates are and what the game looks like, you can create a business plan specific and adaptable enough to allow for the most effective marketing campaign for your target market.

Example: Game plan

The publishing industry is in the middle of a monumental changing of the guard. Large, traditional companies are taking over smaller companies and forming partnerships. This has reduced the number of traditional publishers in the marketplace, at the same time making their portfolios more conservative. Many traditional publishers now limit their authors to influencers with an established following only.

At the same time, small, independent publishers are creating new and exciting content, and taking risks on unknown authors in the hope of finding the next big name that will help them grow their business. In addition, these independent publishers are providing the same quality product as the larger firms due to reductions in cost and advancements in printing.

Share Your Story will offer specialised mentoring programs that meet authors' individual needs. Share Your Story will provide services that create strategies for publication, author branding, marketing and promotion, and giving back.

Market segmentation

Share Your Story will provide services to authors and author/illustrators; however, the business does not take the place of a writers' group, which is an alternative market within the industry. There are many compelling reasons for creative people to turn to Share Your Story:

- Workshops are the core of Share Your Story's success, and bring like-minded people together with innovators in the industry. Not only does this give the participants the opportunity to learn, but they can also find a tribe to support them on their journey to publication and beyond. Share Your Story looks for venues that keep overheads low, and most guest speakers will appear on a voluntary basis. Workshops do not generate large profits; costs cover venue hire, event advertising and catering.
- Share Your Story will focus on publication of work, not peer-based manuscript assessment.

- Events will typically be attended by up to thirty people. These smaller groups will allow for more personalised feedback, and foster continued support and connection via Facebook.
- Online editing services are available for picture-book and middle-grade manuscripts through the website www.sharingyourstory.com.au.
- Experience has shown that authors who use editing services are usually looking for more than just editing as they try to break into the publishing industry. Share Your Story's editors are active in the publishing industry as a whole, and are aware of opportunities and trends. This allows them to offer support and advice on current pathways to publication.

Michelle Worthington will serve authors who want their work published. Share Your Story will educate authors on both traditional and independent publishing options.

Chapter 13

Talk the Talk; Walk the Walk

It will take time for you to make a strategic business plan, set up your author business, promote your brand—both online and in person—and publish your books, either traditionally or independently. This is the side of publishing that many authors are unaware of and struggle the most with.

Being a person of influence in this industry generally means having insight and integrity, and the ingenuity to make it through the tough times. You have a plan in place that will not only make your dreams come true, but also delight your readers, help your peers, and grow the industry for the good of all.

Example: Service statement

We will increase authors' visibility through our website, networking, and participation in fundraising and charity events. Our website will provide in-depth information about the services we offer, and detailed programs of events.

Share Your Story will also be active in giving back to the local and international community by donating a portion of each participant's payment to charities that promote literacy and book giving.

Lastly, founder Michelle Worthington and the Dream Team, a select group of mentor graduates, will be active within the industry, publishing and actively promoting their own books and staying focused on long-term careers. Michelle Worthington will write and publish a book aimed at helping authors market their own books after they have chosen a pathway to publication.

Competitive edge

Share Your Story's competitive edge will be based on two factors: specialisation, and strategic relationships. We will specialise in helping aspiring authors get published. We will also provide contact between authors and large and established writers' groups as a way of providing future support.

Share Your Story realises that once an author is published, they need a different level of support. We believe that our participants will outgrow us, and that is the idea. Applying this philosophy, in addition to providing educational services, we will empower successful participants to become guest speakers at publishing events, and offer training to become mentors or editors. Our educational program is designed with practicality and relevance as the main priority. This allows participants to grow in knowledge and confidence, and gain the necessary skills to operate independently within the industry.

The use of strategic relationships with writers' groups is unusual in the author community. Share Your Story is following the example of companies in other industries that have recognised the value of specialisation and strategic relationships.

Michelle's experience and credentials within the publishing industry, specifically around marketing and promotion, will allow her to successfully self-publish her own nonfiction book.

Sales strategy

Share Your Story will, for the most part, be using the sales strategy of social-media promotion and word of mouth. With ten years in the industry, and two years of consulting for authors seeking publication, Michelle has formed relationships throughout the writing community and publishing industry. Initially, she will leverage these relationships to establish published authors as workshop presenters and mentors. Once Share Your Story has a few successful graduates, Michelle will be promoting them for leadership positions.

Additionally, the Share Your Story website will be used not only to communicate information to prospective participants, but also as a method of communication to provide information on upcoming workshops, author interviews and fundraising activities. It will also be used to sell and promote nonfiction books.

Michelle will be available for speaking engagements on the topic of her nonfiction book, and the development of Share Your Story as a business.

Sales forecast

It is unlikely that there will be any profit within the first twelve months. During the first and second years, Michelle will be developing systems to provide a template for future event planning. Once this is set up, Share Your Story should be able to host workshops easily. The third year should see the start of substantial profit based on income from manuscript assessments, mentor programs and book sales.

Share Your Story offers a superior service at a lower cost due to lower overheads. We will help authors by giving them the knowledge to find pathways to publication within the industry.

Chapter 14

Celebrate the Little Wins

Milestones are important. Celebrate the times when it feels like you're moving forward and getting stuff done. It's as easy as that. It won't always be the case, so take the time to be mindful of your progress. Book launches, other publishing events and sharing with your online community are all ways you can mark the milestones on your journey to success.

I love being part of the process of empowering authors to reach their full potential and see themselves as role models, not only for their families but also for their local communities. I believe there is incredible power in acquiring knowledge, and that everyone throughout the world should have access to quality education. This has become one of the milestones of my business.

Example: Setting the goalposts

- Business-plan completion will serve as a roadmap for the organisation as well as an indispensable tool for ongoing performance and improvement. It will be shared with the tribe at each birthday celebration so the community has a clear vision of what Michelle will try to achieve in the coming year.
- Book launches will be held throughout the country on publication of *Sharing Your Story*, Michelle's nonfiction book for authors on how to promote themselves without the hard sell. There will be champagne.
- Fundraising will supply literacy programs to over one hundred children around the world in the first year, two hundred in the second year, and so on. This will be a key marker of Michelle's success.

Share Your Story will have several early milestones.

SECTION 4

The Power of the Backstory:

Marketing Plan

Chapter 15

Putting the Social into Social Media

It can be extremely difficult for creative introverts to put themselves out there on social media. Instead of trying to be everywhere at once, and not doing a particularly good job of any of the social-media platforms available to authors for promotional purposes, only post where your target market will see them.

To market your book without a big budget, here are some insights and tips to put your title in front of the right audience and increase your sales, develop your branding, and leverage your work without the hard sell. You need to know what product you have to offer to the right person and why it's perfect for them. Include basic information:

- Author name
- Book title
- Book description (a maximum of five to eight sentences)
- Book genres (up to three)

What are the titles and authors of three popular books that are similar to your own? If the book is part of a series, name the series. What two aspects of your title are similar to each of these popular books?

Outreach information:

- Where are you located (city and state)?
- How many libraries are in your area?
- Which non-profit or volunteer groups are you a member of?
- Which business industry would be interested in your book?

Where do you have the most engagement? Do you have a blog? What local media contact do you have?

List your social-media involvement (I have used mine as an example):

- Website: www.michelleworthington.com
- Twitter handle: michelle_author
- Facebook page: https://www.facebook.com/ michelleworthington.author
- Instagram: michelle.author
- LinkedIn: https://www.linkedin.com/in/ michelleworthingtonauthor/
- YouTube: https://www.youtube.com/user/ mworthingtonauthor
- Pinterest: https://au.pinterest.com/ michellewauthor/
- Goodreads: https://www.goodreads.com/ michelle_author

To-do list:

- Register as an author on Amazon.
- Register as an author on Goodreads.
- Create a book trailer.
- Speak on the core topic of your book.

Know your audience. Consider the demographics of the audience you want to read your book:

- Location (city and state)
- Possible non-profit or volunteer groups they are involved with
- Businesses/industries they work in
- Their values
- Their heroes
- Age range
- Gender
- Interests
- Social-media platforms

Chapter 16

Post with Purpose

Each of your social-media posts should have a purpose. Never use the S-word (*sell*). Instead, use any of these magic words in your post—*share*, *give* or *help*—or reconsider your purpose for posting. Social media is not the best place to sell your books; instead, it should be used to build your brand and give followers the information they need to make their own decision about whether to meet you personally for a signed copy, or buy your book online.

Be authentic. Write in the first person in your status updates, and share creative updates regularly. Build excitement around official announcements and promotions, and be industry aware. See what is trending in your network, and set notifications to receive relevant updates in real time. Track what works by following people you admire.

Be where your target market is and understand that people do business with people they know, like and trust. If you have to convince an audience to buy your book, you are in the wrong spot, talking to the wrong people. The purpose behind each post should be of the greatest importance.

Active participation in social media is necessary to help your audience develop both procedural knowledge about what you do—which links the things you do that are in line with your end goals—and schemata, which is having the ability to create in the minds of your audience representations of how your brand fits into the world around them.

Social media is the way the general public acquires, remembers and learns knowledge, with the participant playing an active role in the acquisition process. In this new online world, when we look at others we find both them and ourselves. We are averse to uncertainty and randomness, and prefer coincidence and correlation with our own circumstances.

Your decisions about what to post must be based on logic, prediction, planning and problem solving. To get the target market's attention, you need to process the emotions you assume they would feel, and weigh up the risks and rewards you offer them with each call to action.

Having a nurturing and caring focus rather than a desperate and anxious sales-based approach could mean the difference between your total income and your career longevity in the industry.

The author who gets known for their hard-sell posts is rarely entrepreneurial in their thinking, and often finds it hard to adapt to change. Those who share their knowledge through information—demonstrating emotional intelligence about what is happening in the world of their readers—build relationships that are the foundation of modern marketing.

When many long-term established authors started their writing careers, there was no social media. Today's authors have access to international support groups, forums, and a community that they can pick up and put down depending on where they are in their writing career.

The world of community is not the only benefit that social media offers authors. Previously it was very difficult to find enough information about the publishing industry; now it is possible to find out about other people's experiences, source articles on research, and obtain advice from agents and advocates—all of which can assist in promoting not only your book but also your career.

Chapter 17

Like. Comment. Share.

Online marketing can be implemented in three easy steps. The value of your product, the quality of your product, the price of your product, the characteristics and needs of your ideal client, your marketing strategy, and your overall brand message should all be central to your online and social-media marketing plan.

It can be too easy to get distracted by the 'social' side of social media. Be brave enough to stay on task, and step up to a new level of normal that involves you focusing on making good choices that involve innovation, creativity and change.

1. Regularly share content in effective time slots.

2. Join and become active in peer groups.
3. Encourage followers to like, comment and share your content and page.

Start building your network or pre-position your existing network before your book is released. If you wait until your book is published you will miss out on an amazing marketing opportunity that allows your target audience to go on the publishing journey with you. Making pre-order sales available can help build awareness and momentum, and lead to referrals from readers once they have their copy. Include a thank-you note asking your readers to write a review or recommend it to a friend.

Users connect daily to review their newsfeeds and read about the people they follow, so share elements of your backstory as well as business insights with your network; position yourself effectively as an industry leader on your path to publication.

If you don't have anything to say, you can still share recommended articles, personal insights, corporate presentations, and relevant industry news to demonstrate your knowledge. Make your posts searchable, and available to distribute through other networks, effectively becoming an extension of your professional reputation and, eventually, your book's reputation.

Overcome your objections, if any, to online marketing. Managing privacy on the internet is not a matter of limiting your information; it's deciding what you want to present to those inside your network versus those outside your network. You can easily control the privacy of your network and activities to align with both your constraints and your comfort level by using the privacy options within settings.

A few key points to remember about social media:

- Take part to take control.
- Create an effective profile.
- Control your privacy and confidentiality.
- Connect effectively with the people that matter.
- Be authentic.
- Become a voice for your industry.

Only participate in the social-media platforms you feel comfortable with. It will be exhausting to maintain a presence on social media you don't like, plus it won't have the desired effect and could do more harm than good to your marketing plan. Facebook, in particular, should be used for authentic, engaging posts, not advertising.

Speak from experience, and attract the right people with consistent growth by networking with genuine offers.

Remember that with social media, as with blogging and email newsletters, if you stop, the interest goes away. Create a structured schedule. If you don't like a certain aspect of social-media marketing, don't do it. It will be better to find another way of promotion than do something badly.

Become empowered about your choice of social media so you are in control of what is posted, not constantly reacting to defend your image instead of building it.

Social media isn't intended to replace face-to-face interactions. But it can be invaluable when it comes to optimising your ability to keep your network fresh and active, strengthen global connections, and gain knowledge of the people you have met or are about to meet.

Chapter 18

Don't Believe the Hype

I love to interview successful business people who have written books to boost their credibility, as well as as-yet-unpublished authors to learn about their journeys and how they have overcome obstacles, not only in their businesses and the publishing industry, but in their personal lives as well.

You will face challenges in promoting your personal brand and book. One involves keeping your focus on finding effective ways to promote your brand and book without losing friends. You also need avoid paying too much for ineffective advertising. Interviewing others will not only clarify your own marketing needs, but also help you become associated with well-known, credible and marketable professionals in your industry.

I like to ask questions that can be interpreted in many ways, and questions that open the door to not only informative and interesting answers but also connections that build rapport and mutual respect in the industry. The main question I ask people, more for my own curiosity than anything else, is: How do you find the time to fit everything in?

When I first started my business, there was not enough time in the day to do what I needed to do to get my book written, let alone published, because I spent so much time putting other people first. I worried about being seen as selfish, and felt guilty when I spent my precious time doing things I wanted to do for *me*, instead of for others.

I was constantly questioning myself about whether or not I was making the right decision in investing in myself. I didn't know who was the best person to ask when I needed help in marketing and promotion. I would have liked someone to help me for a change, but I wasn't good at asking for help.

When I ask both unpublished and established authors about what is stopping them from writing, or starting or growing their own author businesses, the answers are nearly always the same:

- No time
- No support
- No money

My next question is obvious: What are you doing about it?

Your time is now

Nobody likes to feel they are letting others down, but if you want to be a successful author and businessperson, you need to get used to putting yourself first … a lot. There is an element of luck and timing involved in success, no matter how talented you are. I have never taken no for an answer when I've been passionate about something (just ask a couple of ex-boyfriends I stayed with for way too long). There will never be a perfect time, but there will be a time when it is too late.

- Learn to say no. Or say 'Not now' if it's something you can see yourself being interested in when the time is right.
- Ignore the phone, or let the answering machine screen calls. Turn off your mobile.
- Plan time for social activities and family life (this is non-negotiable).
- Find a place to work and write where you're unlikely to be interrupted. Leave the house if you have to.
- Close the door if you work and write at home. Put a friendly 'work in progress' sign on the door.
- If someone does interrupt you, stand up; people are less likely to hang around if you remain standing.

Be open to learning what you don't know

You don't know what you don't know, and if you think you already know everything, you will miss out on easier, better and less costly methods of achieving success.

I knew nothing about the publishing industry when started. I knew no one in the publishing industry. I didn't know what to expect, and as a result it took me a lot longer to find success than it should have. I didn't know where to turn for help and I was too scared to ask, being the type of person who always did everything for myself.

I had to change the way I thought about acquiring knowledge from people who had already achieved success. I found groups that offered workshops and classes that could educate me further, and I see this as a valuable investment in my success.

Find the right resources

Many of us have precious little disposable income and free time, especially as authors and business owners who are also caregivers and full-time workers trying to make ends meet. Putting resources into programs and people that are not going to give you the personalised results you need can be demoralising, as well as set back your journey to publication by months, even years.

By researching the resources available to me, I was able to find what best suited my circumstances. I found out which groups to join, meetings I could attend or participate in online, and the type of people I wanted to surround myself with.

These were all personal choices, and you may find other resources that work better for you. Think practically about where you spend your time and money to make sure you're getting the best return on your investment.

SECTION 5

Bringing it Together:

Brand

Chapter 19

Who Exactly Are You?

That this world of ours is full of imperfect people needs no supporting arguments, and there is reason to believe, although we hope for better, that we will not live in a perfect world in our lifetime. Imperfection is a necessity. Celebrating diversity in any industry creates scope for future growth and facilitates smooth transitions as trends change. The past experiences of people from all backgrounds are required to make new paths forward, not just to survive but to flourish.

Human existence is based on diversity and movement, better and worse, light and dark, good and evil. It has its risks and its dangers, and will remain so. The ups and downs save it from stagnation, without which we would not feel fully alive. Don't be afraid to share the good and the bad; it's what makes you human in a world that craves authenticity.

If you are struggling to know where to begin in promoting your book, the first step is to examine your backstory. The second is to practise it until you feel comfortable enough to talk about your story naturally and often. If your backstory fails to connect with your audience, it won't matter how good your products or services are.

Your target market needs to understand why you do what you do. It isn't about selling; it's about finding common ground to relate to your customers so they can understand why what you do is so important.

Your brand outlines why the world will look different as a result of what you will do, and explains that the world is going to feel and look better or different because of the contribution you will make. First impressions count. In a pitch, workshop or even an email, you only have a few seconds to capture someone's attention. It's important to get it right.

The answers to the following questions will give you a better understanding of the *why* behind your business:

- What was your background before you started your business?
- How were you introduced to your business?
- What was the one thing that impressed you the most about becoming a successful author?
- What results have you experienced?
- How is your business making a difference for you right now?

Use the information you gained from these questions in media releases, articles, blogs, company connections. A few additional pointers:

- Communicate just enough about your story that your audience is left wanting to know more.
- Intrigue people, but not so much that they miss the point.
- Your *why* should be compelling and authentic.
- Your *why* should touch upon the most important thing: a reason to consider you as a boss lady.

- A website is the perfect medium. It should:
    - be memorable
    - show why and how you are different
    - make a connection
    - tell the world something about what you're doing in a way that makes people care.

Chapter 20

Why Do I Need to Do This?

Your backstory will build your brand. Sharing your story will create instant differentiation from other people in the industry and allow you to build trust with your customers. Your brand will grow through your connections with people, either online for face to face. From finding a tribe to attracting new customers, it all begins with building a robust following of people who identify with your backstory, and opening the conversation.

Not everyone your meet is going to relate to you and your story, but every connection you make could lead to an opportunity, no matter where you are. Use your backstory to market yourself as a brand, but don't try and market each product or service individually unless you are one of those magical people with more than twenty-four hours in a day.

Sharing your story helps you:

- build relationships
- create brand awareness
- be authentic
- tell people what you are working on
- give respected opinions on articles and current affairs
- add a personal touch.

Your backstory explains why you are committed to delivering quality goods and services. Customers will work with a small business that delivers on its promises over a big brand they don't have a personal association with.

In Australia, bushfires are a yearly occurrence, devouring homes and wasting the landscape. However, certain plant species need the intense heat of these bushfires to release their seeds. The fires are critical to successful reproduction, and without them these species could not flourish. In a similar way, the fires of conflict that pass over our souls can reveal precious gifts before unseen.

Your author brand will suffer if the service and products you give yourself and others are not of the highest calibre. It often takes a costly mistake to understand the importance of this part of the process. No amount of sparkly social media can make up for a badly written or produced book.

By differentiating yourself to others, you create a valuable brand and product. To deliver quality, you will need an understanding of your capacity and value:

- Do you have the support you need to keep your promises?
- Do you have the infrastructure in place to deliver on your promises?
- Having the time, money, knowledge, mission and relevance you need to be successful in your industry is only part of the business plan. Getting people behind the value you are trying to produce is what will truly move you towards a successful marketing mindset.

Backstory forms connections

Modern marketing is about building relationships. Having a compelling backstory along with a collaborate innovation mindset can take your business to the next level. First impressions count. You only have a few seconds to capture someone's attention, so it's important to get it right. Be open to anyone, as every connection could lead to an opportunity to build your business.

Learn to listen for opportunities to bring your business forward, but understand that not everyone is your customer. Sometimes, the connection you make is *through* them, not *with* them, but nevertheless every connection will move your business forward.

Backstory connects creativity to business

The definition of creativity in business is vision with purpose. Use your talent to find new and improved ways to get things done. Just because something has been done a certain way in the past, that doesn't mean it will stay relevant in a dynamic, interactive, digital future. Embracing unpredictability, and finding new ways to engage will lead to new streams of income.

Being open to more than one interpretation of a problem will make you more resilient to changes in the industry, and ensure your position as a person of influence within that sphere. Creativity finds new ways of engaging with your audience. Focus on expressing your creativity through free-value outlets like blogs, videos, social media and newsletters.

The way business is conducted has changed, and it may not be possible for you to continue doing things the way you have always done them. Being creative allows you to become entrepreneurial in your thinking. It means exploring and testing the ways in which you adapt to the world around you, and share your knowledge, in both face-to-face interactions and online. Not all forms of communication work for everyone, so don't try to do everything. Prior knowledge of your target market, and deciding what is the best way of getting your message out to the people who need it most will be your guide to when, where and why you should market your book.

Your backstory explains why you love what you do. Making a difference comes easily to those who are passionate about what they do. Belief in yourself and your work will allow you to find ways to not only help yourself, but to help others with an organic sense of community that makes real change possible in the world.

It is important to find a way to remind yourself every day of what your business means to you, and what it can help you achieve:

- It is deeply personal.
- It is relatable to others.

Backstory helps to create an effective online profile

Across the world, a social revolution is taking place. Driven by advancements in social networking, authors have unprecedented opportunities to connect and interact. Top-performing authors know that social-media engagement is a necessity. They use online networks to achieve a deeper engagement with readers in a high-control, low-risk way.

Broaden and engage in your network by tailoring your profile to reflect your unique backstory. Social-media searches are how potential readers will locate you and understand who you are. Ensure that your website has:

- a friendly profile picture
- a headline that demonstrates your expertise
- posts that engage your readers
- multimedia content to bring your profile to life.

Chapter 21

When Should I Start?

Start targeting your brand *before* you have your first book published. Write down the main ideas and focus of the book so you know who, what and where you should be targeting. It will probably be too late to establish your brand after your book comes out because you will have missed the momentum and shared experiences that a publishing journey can bring.

Your book-marketing plan should include the following information:

- Author name and contact information

- All applicable genres for your book, topic sections, cover design, physical dimensions and page numbers
- One-page summary of the whole book
- Business description in three sentences, i.e. how your book satisfies a need in a specific industry
- Industry background: your experience in the industry or other qualifications
- Competitor analysis: prove there is a market for your book by listing comparable, successful publications
- Target market: which demographic will want your book?
- Media plan for reaching your target audience; for example, social-media advertising, email newsletters, workshops, commercial media contacts, blogs, etc. Will you be entering the book into competitions for further media exposure?
- Distribution: describe the process of creating your book from start to finish, and your plans for distribution. How will you produce your book, and with whom? How will you ensure quality? Who will be your distributor? What plans do you have for distributing the book yourself?
- Financial plan: describe your plan to get funding for the book, the expenses you expect

and how you will recoup the cost over time. When do you think you will make a profit?

When marketing your book, your most important asset is your connection to the reader and how well you know them, as well as how well they know you. If you have no material other than straw, sticks or bricks as a foundation for your marketing plan, then you must use straw, sticks or bricks, and your design and structure will be dependent on that.

Spend as much time on your blurb about the book and the marketing materials as you did on the manuscript.

Compelling product descriptions, preferably with endorsement from other successful authors or business owners, will help your book sell without you having to physically be there to promote it. When people you don't know personally start buying your book, you're on your way to making a profit.

Chapter 22

Where Can I Promote Myself?

B e bold, innovative and imaginative. Establish yourself as the go-to person in your field through your generosity of spirit, as well as being informative and entertaining. A famous musician once played in a metro station without anyone knowing who he was. A few people stopped. Most people walked by—because there wasn't a story associated with him.

The way we tell the story about our work is what makes it worth stopping for. Your intention is not to tell people what they should like, but to make sure they understand *why* they might like your book.

Make it easy for your audience to find you

Narrow down a list of five to seven keywords your audience might typically search for, then incorporate these words into the description headline, description copy, and keyword about-me sections on your website, plus each of your product pages across all your social-media networks.

Once your audience has found you and made a connection, make it easy for them to purchase a copy of your book. You don't want to miss out on sales because of a complicated purchasing or postage system.

Consider an e-book as an addition to a printed copy, but never underestimate the power of being able to hand a prospective participant, partner or client a physical book to take away with them. It will serve as a reminder of your expertise and influence in their industry. A book can become as useful as a business card for getting clients to contact you, and to reduce the need for you to be constantly chasing leads.

Timing is everything. Promote your brand strategically during specifically related events, and when something relevant is trending in the media. Always take advantage of the opportunity to become a part of the conversation, but only in situations where you can and will be viewed as an expert in the field.

'I am ...' is the most powerful start to any marketing journey. Write down your top five 'I am' statements and use them consistently in your promotional copy. A few possibilities:

- I am my target market.
- I am passionate about helping others.
- I am a published author with over ten years' experience in the industry.
- I am a consultant in the publishing industry with a track record of helping authors realise their dreams of being published.
- I am a mother and wife with a close family that is my top priority.

SECTION 6

You Had the Power All Along, My Dear:

Mindset

Chapter 23

Be Relentlessly Resilient

Light and shadow, sunshine and storms are all a part of our lives on Earth. Just as the most valuable steel is tempered in fire, and the strongest trees can put down their deepest roots in strong winds, human suffering can produce greatness of character in those who accept it.

We ask for more than an existence; we ask for a *happy* existence.

For my part, I see miracles everywhere. I see nothing but works of magic. There is a fight to be fought on your own, but you cannot impart goodness to the world unless you're filled yourself, day by day. Place each new day in the loving, strong hands of a resilient mindset, and then you can be all you want to be, as well as give back to the community that supports you and those less fortunate.

Right now you may not have anything that the world considers worth having, or anything of perceived value to give, but if you have a giveback mindset you possess something no money can buy. Approach the future with a sense of sharing.

The one thing light always does is dispel the darkness. You may not always see the path in front of you. Every now and then you have to walk by faith, not by sight. There may still be an element of darkness in your life.

When you first realign your course, the light may seem like the dawning of a new day, growing stronger as you take each new step forward and ever brightening as you find the right track. The more you share this light with others, the more it will guide your own way.

Light, without which the eye cannot function, is comforting to us because it makes everything clear.

We speak of light as 'revealing' and 'illuminating'. Every now and then in our lives, something will happen that reaches us, even if we're in a deep sleep of denial; a cry of warning from the world of realities, and for a moment we're on the verge of waking. Then, when the emotions and the turmoil have passed, we may be tempted to go on living exactly as we lived before. Becoming a published author was my chance to do more than just turn over and mutter in my sleep.

You cannot protect yourself fully from failure, but living with fear will not let you make good decisions about your business. Be accountable for your own success, both personally and with your company and brand, and share your success with others. Set daily and weekly checks to make sure you're on track. Know the numbers so you can improve them, and don't let a feeling of hopelessness make you give up on a life of potential happiness.

A giveback mindset is all about clarity and purpose. If you follow the advice laid out in this book, you will soon be running your business on more than passion alone, and with more passion than ever before. The lessons you learn can help you negotiate a newly revised second edition to your master plan, one that involves giving back to others, if it wasn't included in the first place.

Success and failure don't exist at opposite ends of the spectrum. Success often comes after facing a setback, so learn from the experience and find ways to continually improve. Embrace the fact that you will face resistance or even backlash from your success, but don't let that take away from your joy of giving back to those who have supported you in your journey.

Be open and honest with yourself about what you need to do to make sure you're not setting yourself up for failure before you begin, but make the decision not to let it make you unproductive or despondent.

Don't say 'I'm fine' if you're not; ask for help if you need it. Then let yourself be helped. Open up to people in your close circle of friends. They know you better than you think, and they can give you the emotional support that comes from communicative closeness. Do this solid in the knowledge that when success does come you will be ready and willing to help someone else in return.

You have been given an enduring heart that is able to withstand everything you've been through, with resilience and natural strength to spare. No stranger to bad news, you will not cower or shudder at this, or any further problems. Consider yourself to be a star, a shining point of light in a magnificent celestial universe, someone can provide a guiding light for others.

Could you be a shining light for someone going through the same things as you?

Do you have the opportunity to be a guiding star shining so brightly that people will be drawn to your astonishing optimism?

Do you have the means to be charitable and give others a portion of the proceeds of your success?

Chapter 24

Sharing Is Caring

B ecome part of a support network, and ask for advice or offer assistance. Human experience is an invaluable resource. Be open to new and exciting ways to increase the flow of happiness into your life. Also, be willing to share your knowledge and experience with others to forge a chain that will support them on their journeys. People need the support of others to transition through each phase of their lives. You will work harder if you have your own personal author fan club behind you.

The world has no exclusiveness. It contains everything, provides for everything, welcomes the high and the low, the good and the bad. We human beings are not broadminded: we discriminate, approve and disapprove. Be unconditionally grateful for all that you have in your life.

Having a giveback mindset is not just a fuzzy, feel-good way of thinking; it is a way of life. You have so much to be thankful for. Consciously release any feelings of selfishness, envy or resentment for what you have yet to achieve, and give back to those who have their journeys ahead of them, or who haven't had the same opportunities as you. What you already have is enough to make you happy. Anything more is a blessing.

In the beginning, you may not understand the importance of having a give-back mindset, but as you become part of the amazing community of published authors you will come to see it as an integral part of securing the longevity of the industry.

Life was not designed to be easy, no matter how good or dedicated you may be to becoming a better person. In order to bounce back from adversity and unexpected obstacles, it's important to stay motivated and enthusiastic; helping yourself and others is what will keep you grounded.

- Deliver on all the promises you make to yourself.
- Focus on what you have control over.
- Expect that you're going to make mistakes.
- Respond to mistakes and difficult situations by being committed to the bigger picture.
- Accept responsibility for your actions.
- Apologise for your mistakes.
- Acknowledge your real and perceived limitations.
- Confront roadblocks and challenges with a positive attitude.
- Devise proactive, flexible and unique solutions to problems.
- Focus on what makes you proud of how you handle particular experiences.
- Move forward, taking from the past only that which makes you stronger.

Chapter 25

Build It and They Will Come

From building a team or tribe to finding new readers, it all begins with building a robust following and opening the conversation. Tell your story. Listen to and read about the stories of others. Start conversations with strangers and draw from their experiences.

Rather than looking at this as an exercise to find validation in what has happened to you, or to judge the actions of others, use it to grow stronger in your connections with others. Find a purpose from your past and share it with those who may benefit from the lessons you have learnt.

You know things you never even realised you knew, and by opening yourself up to genuinely care about the wellbeing of others, you will be amazed at the satisfaction you receive from giving of yourself. Practise empathy in everything you do. The capacity for great kindness is innate in all of us, even though not all of us use it.

Your business will grow through conversations with people. Always practise ruthless empathy and find new ways to connect only with your target market. Also, understanding and sharing your experiences with your peers and even competitors will help to grow a robust industry in which everyone profits.

Make yourself more attractive to a wider market by using word-of-mouth endorsements from your connections. Make yourself remarkable through your actions, not just your words. Communication and connection are the new cornerstones of small business.

There are many ways you can use your book to connect with your target audience:

- Speaking engagements
- Workshops

- Online courses
- Social media
- Coaching
- Podcasts

Chapter 26

Learn from the Best

To find their own empowerment, people have endured many things. Mahatma Gandhi, who endured hunger and thirst, said, 'Be the change you wish to see in the world.' Trappist monk Thomas Merton, who meditated in caves, wrote: 'Our real journey in life is interior; it is a matter of growth, deepening and an even greater surrender to the creative action of love and grace in our hearts.'

Han Shan, who is considered one of the greatest Chinese Chan masters and who spent much of his life living alone in the mountains, said: 'The ten thousand things are all reflections, the moon originally has no light.'

In the Byzantine Empire, Stylites (or 'pillar-saints') stood on pillars preaching, fasting and praying. Simeon Stylites preached: 'When we get to wishing a great deal for ourselves, whatever we get soon turns into mere limitation and exclusion.'

To accomplish anything, you need an interest, a motive or a centre for your thoughts. You need a star to steer by, a cause or an idea to follow. There are many different guiding lights to follow.

Nothing was ever done—earnestly and worthily—with half a heart. On every side, the world bears the stamp of the thoughts and genius of great men and women in all the wonderful inventions we use every day. No great works were ever undertaken and brought to fruition by people who were only half-hearted.

Great people have overcome multiple rejections and huge obstacles and gone on to achieve great things. Albert Einstein, the most prominent scientist of the previous century, was initially looking for a teaching post, but after two years of unemployment he took the position of assistant examiner in a patent office. Despite such a lowly beginning, he is now regarded as the father of modern physics.

Nelson Mandela, anti-apartheid activist and winner of the 1993 Nobel Peace Prize, spent twenty-seven years in jail in his commitment to peace and reconciliation.

While she was writing her multi-million-dollar-earning Harry Potter series, JK Rowling was raising a child on her own and living on welfare payments while attending school.

None of these people would have accomplished their great work in the face of great difficulty—and in the case of Nelson Mandela, bitter opposition—if they had gone into it with only half a heart.

Christopher Columbus set sail with a ship, a crew and a star to guide him. Day after day, week after week, he headed west. Winds beat against his ship, seas were heavy, and gales lashed down upon them, but still he headed west. His men threatened mutiny, demanding that the ship be turned back because they were lost, but still Columbus headed west. He had a purpose and a point to prove, and he didn't give up on what he believed in. Finally, after he had lived his darkest hour, he found his way to safe anchorage in the new land that would be called America, changing the world as we know it.

The seaworthiness of the vessel in which you propose to embark should be your first consideration. Are you ready for the proposed voyage with good mental and physical health? It could be a good time to seek the professional advice of your doctor, who may refer you to a counsellor, or put you on a health regime. You can't create an authentic author brand if you're not ready mentally and physically for the demands of promoting your book.

Mother Nature herself shows us every day that change is inevitable. There are now oceans where once there were continents, mountains where once there were seas. From the largest forest to the smallest vegetable patch, everything grows and evolves. Study nature and you discover that air contains oxygen, a magnetic needle points north, and the sun rises in the east and you are warmed. Study yourself, and things may not be so clear-cut.

Without experience, logic can be wrong, and without emotion, nothing is a reflection of the truth. Unfortunately or fortunately, depending on how you look at it, we live in a world that requires constant reinterpretation. Your author brand will change over time, depending on where you are in your career.

Chapter 27

The Right Book, the Right Time, the Right Person

Never underestimate the power of the people you meet on the street, at events or online. Talk with the people around you and be open to how those connections could work for you. Don't see people as just the man at the petrol station, or the woman who delivers the mail. Find out their names and use them to show that these people matter to you personally, and that your interest is not just in the things they do for you. They will be glad to know there's somebody who is interested in them as a person.

What goes around comes around. They might become your biggest and best fans.

But be prepared for rejection so that when it comes, and it will, you already have a way to regroup. Learn from it and move past it. Often the expectation of what it means to be a published author does not match the reality. When the excitement that belongs at the beginning of this new adventure has faded and given way to fact and habit, or when the novelty that gives an author's life its charm has worn off, then comes your true reaction. This reaction is one you have felt before. It might come as a restless craving, a feeling of emptiness, an unsatisfied longing, or a feeling of utter disappointment.

I am very open and honest with the clients I mentor privately. I explain that the descriptor 'published author' may not automatically lead to the advancement they have envisaged.

What you are really seeking in the publication of your book is something you can take firm hold of and say, 'I made this, and nothing and no one can take it away from me.' That requires so much more than just a book.

As a published author, you will be creating a legacy. Your success will not bet measured by the memories you make or even the path you take. It will be measured by what you leave behind. Make sure you are proud of it.

Strategy beats discipline and motivation. Another way to look at it is to think of discipline and motivation as short-term strategies only. Even resilience is a short-term strategy. Practise relentless execution of a scheduled, specific business-and-marketing plan that will take you in the direction of your goals. But be aware that plans, structure and reason can only take you so far.

You heart is where the story is and has always been, beating inside your chest. But mindful of the world in which you live, you may be wary and want to keep your story safe and guarded, hesitant to share too much of your personal past and circumstances.

Think of yourself as you are *now*, not how you were in the past. More importantly, not how you want to be in times to come. You cannot measure the future with today's ruler, or let yourself be held back by the past. Sharing your story is a leap of faith, but it's also a rite of passage.

As a mentor and businesswoman, I want to limit the amount of effort expended by my clients in achieving success, and I do that by giving them a strategy. As a friend, I help them learn, as well as unlearn and relearn. I never want to miss an opportunity to transform the lives of others, and I have found that the most effective way to do this is through my strategic author-business framework.

If you don't try, you will never know, and regret is an awful burden to bear, especially when talent is going wasted. The word I use most often to unpublished authors at my workshops is: 'Try.'

As a mother of three boys, wife of a tradie, fierce lover of literacy, loyal family member and friend, knowledgeable mentor, entertaining presenter, book fairy and pocket rocket, if I can do it, you can do it, too. Don't give up, ever.

About the Author

Michelle Worthington is an internationally published, award winning author of empowering books that celebrate diversity. Yellow Dress Day was shortlisted for the 2013 Crichton Award and featured on Play School. Her first international book Each the Same was published internationally and was a finalist in the 2013 USA Best Book Awards and winner of the 2014 International Book Award for Hardcover Picture Book Fiction and included in Amazon's Top 100 Picture Books for 2014. Hootie the Cutie was the winner of the 2015 International Book Awards for Hardcover Picture Book Award. Noah Chases the Wind was released internationally and was awarded a silver Moonbeam Award for innovation in children's fiction and Gellet Burgess Award for Children's Literature.

Michelle is dedicated to encouraging a strong love of reading and writing in young children and conducts author visits at primary and special needs schools, libraries and bookstore storytelling sessions.

Director of Share Your Story Australia and the Boss Lady Club, she helps aspiring authors all over the world realize their dream of becoming a published author in group workshops, one on one, face to face or Skype sessions and via her online training course, 'Building an Author Business.' She helps writers of fiction or non-fiction plan, edit, submit and market their work to an international market. Authors are encourage to educate and empower themselves to take their storytelling business to the next level by having the right tools, connections and strategies in place to achieve their goals.

She is available for speaking engagements and can be contacted at **www.sharingyourstory.com.au**.

Lightning Source UK Ltd.
Milton Keynes UK
UKHW022147010622
403836UK00010B/1786